CATICORN

Coloring book
for kids

This Coloring book
Belongs to:

....

....

Try Your Coloring Pencil Before Coloring

Try Your Coloring Pencil Before Coloring

Try Your Coloring Pencil Before Coloring

Try Your Coloring Pencil Before Coloring

Try Your Coloring Pencil Before Coloring

Try Your Coloring Pencil Before Coloring

Try Your Coloring Pencil Before Coloring

Try Your Coloring Pencil Before Coloring

Try Your Coloring Pencil Before Coloring

Try Your Coloring Pencil Before Coloring

Try Your Coloring Pencil Before Coloring

Try Your Coloring Pencil Before Coloring

Try Your Coloring Pencil Before Coloring

Try Your Coloring Pencil Before Coloring

Try Your Coloring Pencil Before Coloring

Try Your Coloring Pencil Before Coloring

Try Your Coloring Pencil Before Coloring

Try Your Coloring Pencil Before Coloring

Try Your Coloring Pencil Before Coloring

Try Your Coloring Pencil Before Coloring

Try Your Coloring Pencil Before Coloring

Try Your Coloring Pencil Before Coloring

Try Your Coloring Pencil Before Coloring

Try Your Coloring Pencil Before Coloring

Try Your Coloring Pencil Before Coloring

Try Your Coloring Pencil Before Coloring

Try Your Coloring Pencil Before Coloring

Try Your Coloring Pencil Before Coloring

Try Your Coloring Pencil Before Coloring

Try Your Coloring Pencil

Before Coloring

Try Your Coloring Pencil Before Coloring

Try Your Coloring Pencil Before Coloring

Try Your Coloring Pencil Before Coloring

Try Your Coloring Pencil Before Coloring